WHISPERE[illegible]

A Poetic Journey Through Chaos
to Discovered Dreams

PETER EISSES

This title is also available in Kindle format.

ISBN: (paperback) 979-8-9926304-0-4

Cover design by Benj Mori.
Published with help from 100X Publishing.

Poetry is the song of the soul. Weaving words to explore experiences, emotions, to reflect, to remember—these are our stones of remembrance, our stakes in the ground. With his debut work *Whispered West,* Eisses invites us into his sacred monuments, to explore through his eyes the complexities and beauty of family, faith, and this beautiful life we get to live. Slowly savor each stanza, each couplet, and allow these words to not only be an enjoyable read, but a thoughtful reflection. *Whispered West* just may hold stones of remembrance for you as well.

—Emory Colvin Hornaday, Author of *Seasons Change: A Poetry Collection*, and *Unto Us a Child is Born: A Christmas Devotional*

Experience the creative genius of Peter Eisses in *Whispered West.* This beautiful compilation of poetry puts words to the tension in the journey in life. You will find yourself in these sensational pages, but in a way that you could never have imagined. The fashion in which the words flow together will not only leave you feeling understood, but also overflowing with creativity. This book is one that you simultaneously don't want to put down, but want to savor and sit in each poem. I was overwhelmed with the creativity in these pages and absolutely was taken in with the messages and way the words were woven together. You will not regret time spent in this book, in fact you will cherish it.

—Emily Johnson, Author of *Parents – The Prophets Of The Home*

Peter's poetic voice in *Whispered West* is so unique, like a breath of fresh air for the weary, the contemplative, seekers with questions, and those looking for an oasis of creativity on their journey.

—Krista Dunk, author, publisher, International Prophetic Writers Association and Finding Truth Prophetic Network

Thanks

First, I want to thank my wife, Lisa. I would not be where I am today without you cheering me on. Your beautiful encouragement, amazing questions, and joyful refinement have helped me through the process. This has been a very fun chapter in our great adventure. I love you so much.

Second, I would like to thank all the creatives out there. I love the creative process, whether that is cooking, photography, or building furniture. All things creative have inspired me to write.
There is so much still to be created. Let's keep filling the world with our creations.

CONTENTS

INTRODUCTION

The language of poetry inspires change, challenges thinking, and brings beauty to our world. The poems in this book will undoubtedly do the same. If you enjoy the creative process and the response inside of you as a result of reading creative writing, you will love this book.

Poetry offers creative latitude to convey a message, point, or theme. I think most of us either love or dislike poetry, which I understand. I am fully aware that you may not connect with every piece written in this book. However, I would like to encourage you to look beyond.

With multiple pieces to it, the intent of this book would not necessarily be to read it all in one sitting, although you could if you want. More so, it is meant to be enjoyed over time, one composition at a time, to allow you to experience each poem as bite-sized nuggets throughout the book.

I remember my first memorable encounter with poetry when I was in the seventh or eighth grade. We had been given a few example poems and were encouraged to write our own for an English class assignment.

As a young teen, I was far more interested in football than poetry. Yet, there was a draw toward the way the poet used words to describe that attracted me to attempt a better grade. Looking back, it was also the creative latitude that pulled me in and kept me interested, although I don't think I was able to articulate it then.

I used one of the poems we were given as a general template, and my fourteen-year-old self brought the fire! I received a very high grade for that assignment and was happily impressed with myself because higher grades were not my normal. Unfortunately, the success stopped there. Unable to replicate what I had done in that assignment and not really understanding what had just happened, I dropped the whole thing as a flash in the pan.

Many years later, after a time of processing some directional meetings within a community I was a part of, I picked up writing again and wrote a poem that described the time pretty well. I remember being quite nervous sharing it in front of the community. None the less, it was met with a happy surprise. "Peter! You wrote that?" "Wow, that was amazing." I was rather taken aback at everyone's reaction because in the moment while writing the poem, it flowed quite easily. It didn't feel like a big deal. I was just expressing my process through poetry.

This experience showed me I had the ability to write poetry. The poem I had written when I was fourteen was not just a flash in the pan. It built a slow burning confidence that I had more.

It was around this time when I learned that my grandmother (Beppe) had written many poems as well. Sadly, they were not available for me to see because they had been lost or destroyed. She was untrained, and English was not her first language. Nonetheless, I sure would like to have read them. The realization that writing and poetry had been a part of my family's journey helped me embrace my creative process and gifts.

The creative process is as unique as there are people, and the use of words in creativity is no different. It goes without saying that words are powerful. They have the amazing ability to illicit action and emotion. They are passionate, savage, and just. And when expressed in a creative manner such as poetry, they have the ability to bring change.

My process of creating poetry mainly comes when I am processing situations and events. It might be a small thing I notice that piques my interest or a larger life event or a struggle I have been tackling.

I have discovered the importance of this for myself; it is an incredibly important way I can get stuff out of my heart and mind. Poetry is a way for me to express and communicate much of the sometimes-jumbled feelings and emotions that are either log jamming my journey or are seemingly random pieces of my puzzle I am figuring out. All of us do this on one level or another and in many different forms. Poetry is one of mine.

Most of my work uses the power of rhyme and placement of words. Some of my inspiration has come from the spoken word genre. Much of my work is similar to spoken word poetry and can be read as such.

When I was writing many of these poems, the best way to describe the process would be this: A phrase or a single word would pop into my mind. Other words that related to it would start to flow, horizontally, vertically or like a river around the initial thought. The words seemed to resonate with a rhythm and movement in my head. Sometimes it feels like a dance.

Communicating this dance is part of my expression. Within the communication is often an emotion and passionate intensity that comes through. You can set a metronome to many of these poems.

As you read, allow the words to dance in your mind. Let them impact you, stir up your emotions, and hopefully bring clarity to you. Many of you will be able to identify with what is being written. Enjoy reading my process.

Cheers,
Peter Eisses

Throughout this book, you will see QR codes at the end of certain poems. Use your smart phone to visit these links, and listen to Peter Eisses reading those poems via his YouTube channel.

To visit Peter's YouTube channel directly, go to:

www.youtube.com/@PeterEisses

SECTION ONE

A Perfect Storm

I believe many of us are trying to enrich and better our lives. Whether that is through going to the gym, reading self-help books, or learning from our mistakes, along the way to betterment, alignment happens. This one word *alignment* has helped me through much of my process and journey.

Alignment speaks of making adjustments, bringing order into chaos, or new positioning. All these and more have defined much of where I've been and I'm sure where I'll visit again. To fully appreciate the calm, you will have had to experience a storm.

Whispered West

In the tangled unrest.
Of soul distressed.
On my knees request.
For a life vest.

Heart beating out of chest.
Yet pressed.
With much express.
This be the quest.

It is there confessed!
Sometimes depressed.
Often suppressed.
In a blue moon oppressed.

The uninvited guest.
Would suggest.
This infest.

Out from under the passed test.
And into the nest,
Of rest.
To digest.
This reinvest.

There assess.
What be the acquiesce?
Of such manifest?

A request!
The Voice impressed.
A gentle command, expressed.

It Whispered, *West.*
There under the tree of zest.
Addressed.
Attention arrest.

Be blessed.
In this new dress.
No longer a guest.

Align

The old is becoming new.
Paths are coming into view.
Your desert, that has been normal and true.
Is now on the brink of kissing the dew.

When we align ourselves with Him.
Sometimes He takes us to the outer rim.
To show us things that are far from thin.
To get us thinking of the greater win.

At times we are distant from joy and glee.
Here is where I make a plea.
Come to Me.
So you can see.
Here I be.

Great the angles of decision.
Far from the eyesight vision.
More the distance driven.
Endless the time addition.
Providing all of provisions.
Deep the love condition.

Come to the surface, you of tarry and flew.
You who feel forsaken and blue.
The forgotten too.
The One, the only, He fore knew.
Yes! The old continues to be made new.
Let me sum up and say, this is more than true.
The future is full of me and you.

Here we go, on up too.
I hope these words will cause you to stew.

Design

By design.
Our purpose refine.
Lay it all on the line.
To find.

We climb.
Up the incline.
Ready for redesign.
On a journey of refine.
To find the shine.

Through peril and pine.
Grime and whine.
Brine and malign.
Down to the core and the spine.

Here we supine.
Like grape on the vine.
Out of the confine.
Knowing it's time to assign.
The correct combine.

Fire lit by tinder and tine.
It's going to be fine.
To become entwine.
Take up the pen and sign.

Realize the align.
Here, a new define.
Up the incline.

To the ultimate mine.
We wine.
We dine.
Rest and recline.
With our King the Divine.

Adjust

Get past this a must.
The fence of mistrust.
Has caused a bitter crust.
Need to adjust.
Discuss.
Before we are dust.

Where to start?
Miles apart.
Stains known by heart.
Where the depart?
What will be the jumpstart?
To impart?

Blackboard.
Chalkboard.
Billboard.
Keyboard.
Dartboard.
Switchboard.
Clipboard.
Can we be one accord?
Get aboard.

Love does not record.

It continues to sound.
All around.
Astound.
Profound.

Will not be drowned.
Will not be bound.
Cannot impound.
Calling homebound.
To be crowned.

Forgive the knockdown.
Clampdown.
Lockdown.
Crackdown.
Shutdown.
Breakdown.

We will.
Freedom our hill.
Our forefathers did instill.
Fought for the bill.
Even blood they did spill.

Of great concern.
Is this turn.
Continue to return.
And not adjourn.
Until love does again burn.

Shine

It's time to shine.
Not pine.
On the grind.
Of purpose and find.
Go get immersed in some new wine!
I promise, it will be fine.

This is the time.
To take the climb.
Up and over prime.
Through the grime.
And past the rhyme.

The mountain incline.
Need to be remind?
That part of the align.
Was signed.

At the top of what was mined.
Is a table to be dined.
Fully lined.
With all of everything, kind.

When looking in the review, behind.
The realization, much has been defined,
And refined.

The bell has been chimed.
Feet now reclined.
Fully realigned.
Unwind.

Pay Attention, Listen

Listening to the rumor.
Without humor.
Quick as a schooner.
Often in the hour, lunar.
Vicious as a tumor.

Spread.
With fear and dread
Wishing for dead.
Many words not said.
Unread.
Uncarefully tread.

Shaking the minds of women and men.
When!
Listening to the deceptive voice within.
Over and over again.

Where's the oxygen?

Feeling unstable.
Are we able?
To reach through the fable?
With what's on the table.
Disable.
Tear off the label.
It may be fatal.

Is the sample.
A strong enough example?
To wrangle.

The ensuing scandal.
With a gamble.
To tangle.
The words may strangle.
With the ability to mangle.
Don't leave it dangle.
Read the preamble.
Light a candle.

Aye!
The hour is closer than nigh.
It doth intensify.
Longing to be in the identify.
Don't live in disqualify.
Untie.

Good company with you, many alumni.
Exemplify.
Help you apply.
Steer you from the awry.
Undo the tongue tie.
Don't preoccupy,
I'm just junior high.
You qualify.
Own and verify.
An unending supply.
Make it solidify.
Spread unto and electrify.

Oh my!
Hear the cry.
Make you fly.
You'll know why.

Hurdle

How verbal.
Are you about your hurdle?
Out of the circle.
Is the soil fertile?

Are you the carrier.
Of your own barrier?
Making it harrier and harrier.
Hyper than a terrier.

Inferior,
In your interior?
Superior,
In your exterior?

Does your belief.
Bring grief.
Because it's a thief?
Need relief?

What action?
Will gain traction?
From the distraction.
The infraction.
Over-reaction.
Break faction.
For a new transaction.

Call an audible.
It's possible.
Solvable.
Optimal.
To clear the obstacle.

What information.
Will be used in this situation?
Furthering the conversation.
For greater participation.
Creating determination.
For cooperation.

In you is the outcome.
Deep inside it will come from.
Here you become.

All I Need

All I need to succeed.
Dream.
All placed here right at my feet.
So much here, how could I feel incomplete.

A maze of love encourages me.
Circles of paths radiate from the revelations that shore me.
A deep affection guides me.
Moving me away from myself.
Into the arms of Truth.

I'm crowned by a throng of voices, yet very few heard.
I'm loved by a deepening love that I really don't deserve.
I'm seated at a feast, where joy unexpected, peace unexplainable, hope undeniable are served.
I'm a son in a palace court, with keys for more doors and windows than I can observe.
All placed at my feet for me reserved.

Blend

Playing the game.
Of coffee and claim.
What's the aim?
To wake from the shame.
The same.
The blame.
The ambition, that's lame.

Where is your dream?
That makes you gleam.
Maybe extreme.
Yet flows in your bloodstream.
Weightier than a beam.
Brighter than a sunbeam.
Make you want to swim up-stream.
Jump up and down, scream.
And rule supreme.

Time to install.
Answer the call.
Pick up the windfall.

It may be abrupt.
This, the construct.
However, the risk is worth the erupt.

Evidence states.
The longer the wait.
The more on the plate.
Longer the date.

Thinner the ice skate.
Embrace the new place.
Run a new race.
Fly to a new space.
Start a new pace.
Gaining the base.
To encase.

Yes, resonate.
Open the door to the sound, orchestrate.
Boil the pot, percolate.
Seasoned to perfection, marinate.
Remove the walls, renovate.
Ask the questions, collaborate.
Put it all the table, evaluate.
Get out the spreadsheet, calculate.
Join a movement, rejuvenate.
This navigate.

Here at the end.
May this amend.
Be our send.
To a new game, new dream, blend.

The Wall

Got some walls that need to come down.
Hiding me from being found.
Finding myself bound.
Truly confound.

Mind in impound.
Housebound.
This compound.
Forced underground.

Light in the tunnel.
Opened up like the chunnel.
Peaceful like the backyard runnel.
Need hammers no more, pummel.

Here's where it all started.
As the departed.
New maps charted.
Parted.
Remembering the mortar, smarted.

It's all right.
In this new light.
Reaching new height.
Out of site.
What a delight.
This flight.

The wall gone.
In this new dawn.
Opportunities work on.
Toss out the coupon.

Not long ago.
Did I see this rainbow.
Earlier I wish the memo.
Nonetheless, let's go.

Bliss

Through the mist.
Hands raised high, unclenched fist.
Stood bliss.

Silence split.
Mind, blitz.
Emotion, mix.

Today, met Bliss.
It would be remiss.
To not describe this.

All the markings of one first kissed.
Tattoo on the wrist.
"I Belong" can't miss.

Difficult to predict.
Even harder to script.
However, it sticks.

Beyond joy twist.
Never quits.
Deep in reminisce.

High above the cliffs.
With heights persist.
Speaking with convict.
You may need some, assist.
It grips.

Is this a myth?
Shall I resist?

Gone is the conflict.
The sting and the hiss.
I suppose tossed in the abyss.

Get all the gets.
All the bits.
All the fits.
All the hits.
Yet here it remains, it sits.

Ready for a commit.

Here, a challenge, a risk.
So easy to dismiss.
Say it with me, put it on your lips!

Bliss.

Clean Up

Don't stop.
The momentum is real, it's been rolling for days, nonstop.
The message is clear, gaining altitude, all the way to the top.
Causing some to flip and some to flop.

Tears of the free.
Falling for you and for me.
Guarantee.
I think you will agree.
There were more than two or three.

Stored in a tin.
Fortunately for us it was thin.
Tears soaked the ground, there it did begin.
Awaking a giant deep within.

This giant was laid.
When our country was made.
Thank God they all stayed.
They weighed and they prayed.
Understanding those afraid.
Pressing on, knowing this was an upgrade.

The call, the sound.
Makes your heart pound.
Want you to jump up and spin round.
Around and around.
Calling to be found.

Response is clear.
All come near.
Where there is no fear.
The One will steer.
And catch every a tear.
Lead us to a new frontier.

Freedom is ringing.
There from the beginning.
Keeps us clinging.
To the land of living

Here, there's no shame.
No blame.
No lame.
Many here came.
Hearing their new name.
Spoken long ago, to claim.

Don't stop.
No time to swap.
Get out the mop.
And set up shop.

Co

Hitch yourself to Me.
Hanging on the tree.
The highest fee.
Blood gave the guarantee.
We are free.

Days count them—one, two, three.
Deeper than the sea.
Buried, we.

The appointee.
Got the key.
For you foresee.

Death could not hold me.
Oh, the glee.
The beginning of a new jubilee.

A new decree.
Foresee.
Heaven bound, new ID.

Your seat is my seat, I see.
All of us, the invitee.
To be a new addressee.
Adoptee.

Hitch yourself to Me.

Collision

We are living deep in the land of decision.
A new era, through out, full of new provision.

Ones that need much precision.
So as not to cause division.

As we rise daily appear before us new revision.
Let's remember, it's here we are because of history's collision.

We live in times of excision.
Words, acts, plots, thoughts of derision.

In all of us there is a deep incision.
The scar remains to examine without supervision.

Here as understanding comes, I do envision.
A future will emerge of how hope won and created new vision.

Dual

Cock-a-doddle doo.
Wake up, get up its 2022.
Lots to think through.
More to put in the queue.
Stew.

Before the "O bother" of Pooh.
Conclusions drew.
Imaginations flew.
Negativity spew.
Brew.

Here in the land of the canoe, ski-doo, and snowshoe.
Before the words get any more black and blue.
We need breakthrough.

Some feel we are on a path of deja vu.
One or two.
Settle for a game of peekaboo.
Other travel down a different avenue.
Misconstrue.
All feeling worse than stomach flu.
It's about revenue!
Internal review!
A big hullabaloo.
What's your world view?

Out of the blue.
It's been in our purview.
Time to put on the other shoe.

Share a fondue.
Walk the morning dew.
Play some horseshoe.
Get out and barbecue.
Enjoy a home brew.

We need more than "make-do."
To subdue.
All that's askew.

Here's a walk-through.
Pursue, review.
Turn to.
Undue.
Look into…
New angle of view.
Rendezvous with peer review.

Where is the glue?
That is our run into.
Heartier than beef stew.
Quicker than growing bamboo.
Sweeter than honeydew.

We need its re-debut.
Get out the corkscrew.
Uncap and bring into.
Full view.

Hope anew.
Will renew.
Bringing a new point of view.
Field of view.

Overview.
All that will ensue.
That is tried and true.
Will remain, I knew.

For our freedom to continue.
It's up to us to follow-through.
This old but new.
Connective tissue.

Ever Feel This Way?

The barometer's rising.
Storm's a coming, surprising.
Take cover advising.
Rain baptizing.

The wind is a howling.
Water is drowning.
Biting and scowling.
Prying and prowling.

Many are frowning.
Red in the accounting.
Deshingled the housing.
Bills be a mounding.

Caught mouthing.
Shouting.
Doubting.
My vowing.

They say in a storm.
Heroes are born.
Hard to believe when you feel so torn.
Worn.
Internally Scorn.

Hard to even yawn.
Withdrawn.
Feel like a pawn.
Gone.

"Pick up the pieces," they say.
"Tomorrow's another day."
Go away!
Leave me to survey.

Look for the okay.
The sun ray.
And a way.
Out of this grey.
Delay.

Faithful Is the Sun

At 8:01, up came the sun.
The very first of 2021.
Proving yet again the loving love of the Son.
Showing us how it's done.

This will be a year of reclamation.
For you, your family, your nation.

It still not too late, the train has not left the station.
I know it can still feel like, "I just need a vacation!"
But, you know? Take this into consideration!
From the very beginning of creation.
This moment! This time! Has been for you, your preparation.
My friends, new revelation!
Let that be your destination.

So, in this new year!
Let's make it a point to eliminate the fear.
And pioneer joy and good cheer.

First Love

Where is the love?
I know it's not far.
Quite close, in fact.
That first love!
The undeniable kind.
The gooey kind.
The sloshy kind.
The trip over your own feet kind.

It wants back.
You may have thought it left.
But it didn't.
It has been there all along.
Waiting...
Waiting patiently to resurface again.
Waiting faithfully for engagement again.
Waiting for rediscovery.
It beckons to you.
Come back.
I'm over here.
Not far. Not far at all.
Right there.
Right there in your memory.
Deep inside, those memories have not faded.
Or failed.
They remain.
Like guideposts to our future.
First Love.
Let's get back to First Love.

SECTION TWO

Dream

All of us have dreams and aspirations, whether big or small. Some may seem impossible and grand. Some are points along the way, and as they happen, it occurs to us that *this is a dream of mine.* Dreams are meant to be fulfilled—not undone with the taste of disappointment. Let's continue to dream and inspire each other to go hard after them because dreams were given to us to point us in the direction of fulfillment.

Five

It's four eleven.
Sitting in Heaven.
All heart, no leaven.

Much has been given.
Much forgiven.

Allow it to set in.
Glisten.
With what has been written.

Out of prison.
New dawn risen.
New songs listen.

This condition.
Here, new edition.
New position.

Which of the five.
Will be your jive?
Where you thrive.
Your drive.

One sent.
Answer the call went.
Maker of tent.
Bring repent.
With new invent.
Augment.

Hear the bell.
What did it spell?
Did it yell?
These foretell.

Dig deep into the well.
For a future to swell.

Any cost.
For what is lost.
Those tossed.
Caught in permafrost.
A heart soft.
Caught.

Comfort in the disaster.
All things matter, closely factor.
Even the captor.
Speaking chapter after chapter.
Love and laughter.
Here forever after.

Understanding to the lines, preach.
Crack the code, breach.
Often in eloquent speech.
Build on foundations, concrete.
Complete.
Unleash.

Did one arrive?
In taking the deep dive.
Alive?
In the hive.

Revive.
This is the turn.
Where we learn.
To burn.
To discern.
To yearn.
You will earn.

Fly

I believe I should fly.

When the glass has been broken.
And all the words spoken.
Ask...
What have I done?
Where have I gone?
Did I move?
Did I answer the invitation?
Of higher?
Or did I just take the flyer?
What did I?
Create...?
Make...?
Who did I...?
Date?
Rate?
Fake?

I know I should fly.
Because by and by.
There is completion.
In the decisions I make.
There is dancing and grove.
There is rhythm and move.
This I do not overstate.

All the questions
Cause one to ponder and think.
This, I need a drink.

Here…
I learn the truth.
I am nothing without You.
I am everything with You.
Possibly…
Everything gone in a blink.

I know I will fly.
The greats of this earth.
Your campions of merry and mirth.
Also know.
Your potential.
Your value.
Your purpose.
Your worth.
Here?
Here I fly.

For a Friend

Come near.
Lend me an ear.

It's the season of nearer and nearer.
Never been more clearer.
Put away the mirror.

The ship will be a self-steerer.
The more the hearer and hearer.

This is the year.
When all the work, the tear.
The long staring off, peer.
The fear.
The sneer and jeer.
Will no longer rear.

But will draw near.
A new veer.
Kicked into high gear.

New financier.
Not cavalier.
But sincere!
Further than Tangier or Zaïre
See the cashier.

Its crystal clear,
This engineer.
Did interfere.

Reappear.
The beauty of chandelier.
Said the auctioneer.
Older than a musketeer, buccaneer,
Privateer.
No mutineer.
Here.

A New frontier
Cheer.
Will make its premier.

More than a sightseer
Pioneer.
So much more than a souvenir.
Will commandeer.

The persevere.
Clear.
No more volunteer.
To puppeteer.
Domineer.

Pick up the spear.
This career.
With fresh veneer.
Will adhere.
Endear.
More than mere.
A whole new sphere.

Fourteen

The days are four and fourteen.
Ones spoken of and foreseen.
Landing in a magazine.
And on the big screen.
Days like no one has ever seen.

Do I have your attention, are you keen?
Hope is green.
In the here and in between.
It's your time, in your make-up, your gene.

Out of the can, sardine.
Climb the ravine.
Break the routine.
Get out of the self-imposed quarantine.
Stand up to the machine.
And jump into the unseen.

Come and glean.
Into your new season, clean.
Off the milk, wean.
To a new cuisine,
Protein.

Saved from the guillotine,
Of the has been.
And the Frankenstein,
Routine.

Accept no lien.
No average, no mean.
No character, demean.

Increase the dopamine.
A shot of caffeine.
From the finest bean.

Past the smokescreen.
That appears obscene.
There is a new scene.
From the experience glean.

There is a better view on the mezzanine.
Here, reconvene.
Prepare the limousine.

Dreams

Spent the day with friend out in the heat.
Taking it to the streets.
Listening to the dreams of others, discrete.
What a treat.

Hearing one of the many ways Creator speak.
Some incomplete.
Stuck on repeat.
But mostly just truly sweet.
Most memories concrete.

There was evidence of deceit.
That tries to cheat.
With images and fear conceit.
Lies exposed defeat.
Put on notice, delete.
You are beat.
No need to compete.
For love is complete.
And will not take second seat.

Left with hunger, eat.
Understanding that the need is great to meet.
It is time to face this feat.
And spread the seeds as the wheat.

Move On

Put on a groove.
And prove.
Your thoughts behoove.
That indeed it's time to move.

What will be the choose?
Follow the clues.
The news.
The reviews.

The cheer in the air.
Many a prayer.
A bit of dare.
A snare,
Here and there.
A little scare,
Of the new where.
And maybe, even a tear.

There is an assume.
It could make room.
Stay, be that loom.
The whom.
Lower the boom.
Feels like doom.
Time to get out the broom.

Pick up the stone,
That was thrown.
Get on the phone.

Away from the alone.
To what's known.
What's been shown.
Our backbone.
Comes from the throne.

Enough is enough.
Yes, at times rough.
Put on the tough.
Grab life by the scruff.
This dream will not snuff.

Before me a scene.
Of pastures green.
A new routine.
The cuisine!
Oh yes, keen.
At times it may seem.
To be unseen.

Weighed in the balance.
The palace.
The valance.
And all the talents.

Looking from the prow.
Of the now.
At all the wow.
And the how.
This was an endow.
So, will I allow.
This new vow?

Up

The Journey can be tough.
Rough.
Feel like not enough.
Handcuff.
Blow out the candle, snuff.

Question?
Was it transgression?
Oppression?
Not enough confession?
The wrong impression?
Just depression?
Bad indigestion?
Stopped up congestion?

This quest.
Is it a test?
Guessed.
Pressed.
Stressed.

Where to go?
To get more info.
Out of this sideshow.
Don't want to be a John Doe.
On this march out of the domino.

Out of this pit.
Shown the hit.
The counterfeit.

The slit.
The split.
The nit

Just sit.

Admit.
Probably need a bit.
Some grit.
With more than wit.
New permit.
On it.
Will not submit.
To quit.

Mount up, mountain.
Beautiful fountain.

Prepare for the count down.
All around.

It's been sounded.
Surrounded.
Asking to be founded.

Much to be encountered,
Accounted.
Must be empowered.
Showered.

Once in the carriage.
Will not disparage.
This new marriage.

Fueled Up

Fueled up and ready to go!
The buckle, hello!
Turn the key and make those plugs glow.
Time to reach a new plateau.

Much acceleration ahead.
Use that foot of lead.
Leave some tread.
Some ash fault to shred.

The engine is running!
It's purring and humming!
And the view is just stunning.
The drums are a drumming.
The strings are a strumming.
The sight clear, where this is summing.

The door swung wide open!
And something was awoken.
Here's hope'n.
Nothing will be broken.
But for sure words spoken.

The launch came from within.
As soon as you got in.
And knew when.
It was time to begin.

There wasn't much choice!
You lost your voice.
The eyes moist.
Arms raised in rejoice.

It was time to move forward!
This is just what the doctor ordered.
Out of the office cornered.
Over the border, northward.

There is no turning back!
Get out in front of the pack.
Onto a new track.
Out of the lack.

No time to go slow.
Get out of the flow.
And into the know.
New horizons to grow.

Let's go!

Haze

Out into the sun, gaze.
The weight of last season's maze.
Melts quickly away in a blaze.
Along with the delays.
All the craze.
The seeming nonstop haze.
The winding road that sometimes betrays.

The warmth of the rays.
Of newness amaze.
Awaken the lengthening days.

I must know these ways!
Before my mind strays.
And drags me back to the malaise.

This will be what pays.
Add to the weight, weigh.
It's a case of the Fridays.

I seek no praise.
No accolades.
Not a holiday.
Or the seemingly better yesterday.

Just clarity in the grey.
Sun to make hay.
A sense of always.
And a full tray.

Coffee and Cream

On a late winter's eve.
To the pillow did cleave.
Getting up to perceive.
Something unreal, hard to believe.

A picture thus begun to interweave.
Initiating a path for the mind to receive.
Where did this conceive?
Am I naive?

It started as a seed.
Long ago decreed.
In the secret of creation, agreed.
Built to succeed.

It's more than what may seem.
With more than one theme.
A feel of redeem.
As real as coffee and cream.

Just breathe.
Get the thoughts out, not the time to sheath.
Let 'em run, stampede.
Not the place for aspirin, teethe.

Clarity is in need.
Spirit, lead.
Imagine with an urgency, speed.
To raise this idea, the moment seized.

Get up and make it into a read.
Proceed.
Before it is overgrown with weeds.
And gets lost in the reeds.

Feels somewhat incomplete, guaranteed.
Work and massage it, precede.
Living there, in my mind plead.
Obstacles out of the way, they do impede.

None the less, let see where it leads.
Push past the fatigued.
The schedule besieged.
Expectations exceed.

Send it out to be screened.
Review, rewrite, edit, then reconvene.
And with the pressure appeased.
Opening teased.

Far too long, it seemed.
The final product fully dreamed.
Birthed, fully out in the open, breathed.
Let it be decreed.

High Noon

When Love enters the room.
There is no doubt, no doom.
No place to assume.
Or presume.
The sweet smell of perfume.
Long foretold in the womb.
Conquer of the tomb.
Our destiny won and will play its tune.
Out from the desert dune.
From the rock hewn.
None too soon.
Set free from the cartoon.
The once in a blue moon.
Released from the cocoon.

The invitation sent out, to commune.
With our Groom.
Because it is high noon.

I Claim

Get in the game.
A new place, a plane.

Remove the same.
The boring and plain.
The striving and strain.
I feel the drain.
More than maintain.
Stake a claim.

I see Zion's rain.
Flow like the lion's mane.
No pain.
Better than champagne.
I ascertain.
Here find sustain.

In this new terrain.
Learn to abstain.
From vain and mundane.

I will not waver and wane.
Move me you will not, not even a crane.
New life attain.
Much here to gain.
Here, I reign.

It's Often More Than it Seems

Falling through the mist.
In a gentle twist.
With no assist.
Everything touched, kissed.

Their falling hard to predict.
Here and there, clicked.
But fully equipped.
For the script.
Of the slipped.

This is what was wished.
Others shake their fist.
Learn to coexist!

Their persist.
Is not something to resist.
Everyone dismissed.
Flashing lights enlist.

White gold gift.
Shaped in drift.
All mixed.
As drivers down shift.

Sit,
For a bit.
With warm mitt,
Knit.
Remaking the kit.

Must Omit.
Admit.
It's not time to quit.
But get into it.

Many may be split.
Over this transmit.
However, submit.

With a melt legit.
It's often start, a small slit.
Spring is lit.
Hope emit.

Promise

Here we go.
Greeting ready for a deep overflow.
Hear the rustle of gentle wind blow.
A fire that burns, not too hot, not too slow.
On earth, we sow.
Building a legacy in which we can stow.

A place where no enemies ploy.
Will be able to seek or destroy.
For that matter...also neither meddle nor toy.

Not ambushes that suddenly appear.
Not fear.
Not jeer.
Nor meager or mere.
Not tears.
Not too many beers.

Far from all the bizz.
The whir and whiz.
Way beyond earth's sphere...it is.
Because it lives.

Long above our breath.
Deep, deeper depths.
Further than forgotten stresses.

Higher, highest heights.
Mighty, mightily might.
Further than the furthest sight.

Way beyond all the test.
Better than our bestest best.
Tastier than the tastiest zest.

Simply, blessed.

SECTION THREE

Seasons

Having spent most of my life on the farm, the seasons are very much a part of my every day. Observing them became much more than just a random occurrence or an occasional thought. No, it has become part of who I am. And even, at times, seasons defined me.

Seasons

Out here on the farm.
Away from hectic harm.
The birds your alarm.
Quiet charm.

The lessons of the season.
Will speak to your reason.
Bring completion.
To the questions that feel so uneven.

The tension of transition.
Will reveal its position.
Its mission.
Is a multiple doubling addition.

The seed when planted is buried and dies.
Soon after a few days will rise.
To a much bigger size.
Reaping a greater prize.

The divine cry.
Certainly, did supply.
The answers to *why*.
There is no deny.
No possibility of lie.
When a sprout reaches high.
High up in the sky.
The reason to miraculously testify.
There's no doubt on Whom I must rely.

Summer brings much strength and growth.
Some rest in the sleepy warmth, both.
Embrace the sun's oath.

Harvest always will come.
When the heat of sun.
Has relented some.

The work will increase.
No time to release.
No cease.
Until finished, then peace.

The seasons they do speak.
And yet all have a peak.
Strengthening our physique.
Even though we may feel antique.
Waters the week.
Even when it feels bleak.
Here leave you in this journey, continue to seek.

Autumn

The seed sown now complete.
Has taken its seat.
And is now ready to eat.

Arise, take to your feet.
Come from the street.
From poor to elite.

Send out the tweet.
Come to the harvest meet.
It is replete not petite.

The pace may not be neat.
No matter sun, snow, rain, sleet.
Finish and winter beat.

This be the reason entreat.
To accomplish this feat.
Looking for the final receipt.

Spring

The warm rays of the sun.
Bring the babble of the brook run.
Yes, it has begun.

Green hits the homerun.
The robin's song sung.
Spider's web spun.

Life in its bull-run.
Like a shot from gun.
Cause the look of stun.

The beauty will not succumb.
Light and photosynthesis won.
The sound of insect's hum.

Growth measured in ton.
Long hours with the son.
Will not be undone.

Summer

Heat makes it clear.
We are in another gear.
Jump into refreshing off the pier.

Waves on the horizon appear.
Shimmer on the road unclear.
Beckoning a new frontier.

Work is here.
Sunburn your souvenir.
Water melts, disappear.

Expansion is the steer.
Lack in our rear.
This, the persevere.

Do not waver or veer.
The promise of fruit we do peer.
It's time to stand and cheer.

Winter

The wind blew.
Three days and nights of complete white stew.
Retreat to the coach to review.

Rest brings renew.
It is tried and true.
Often overdue.

Trees naked in full view.
Fingers and toes bleu.
As the blade cuts through.

Last season's extra growth undo.
There's much to do.
Facing the revenue.

As Spring drags its pursue.
The cold is what's needed to pass through.
Making all new.

Known

Late in the night.
His voice speaks so clear it brings clarity and light!
Calling to your depths much to your delight.
Releasing a love that is an unexplainable sight.

What a commotion,
Deep within, stirring up so much emotion.
Here, finding more will for devotion.
With the promise and hope of a gathering promotion.
A love that is deeper than any ocean.
Oh, what a soothing motion!

The Way Out

We all need a good laugh.
A quote, an engrave, oh yeah, an epigraph.
So, on behalf.
Of my gaffe.
Armed with a bar graph.
Raise the carafe.

To my thoughts, they sometimes feel like chaff.
But reach toward new heights, my friend giraffe.

Grab the shaft.
Of the staff
The one you did craft.
Your whole, not half.

These words do submit.
To bridle and bit.
Worked on the wit.
Did not quit.
Went to the pit.
To be refit.
Must not omit.

On the way out.
Found a new route.
With a little pout,
Did spout.
However, gained some clout.
In that drought.

There must be a respond.
In this upward beyond.
Correspond.
Then it dawned.

Review the scan.
The plan.
You know, the one from Stan.
Or was it Dan?
Peter Pan?
Doesn't matter, it came at the beginning of this race, ran.
The one from your clan.
The biggest fan.
It says you are a new man.

Making Hay

Miracles are today.
And are about to go on greater display.
There won't be a delay.
So, look up and eliminate dismay!
Believe, before the month of May!
Make a way.
Shine they will, like sun's rays.

What do you say?
Nay?
Yay?

Out of the sandbox, no more play.
It is time to make hay.
And send the foe into disarray.
He will rue the day.
He tried to make us pay.

This is the season, where we celebrate the baby in a manger lay.
I say, "Eh!"
"This is the way!"
Miracles today!

New

Undoubtedly, we live.
In a time sometimes combative,
Restrictive,
Even resistive.
Determinative.

To the top elbowing.
Words throwing.
Around in circles rowing.
Where are we going?

The culture maker.
Is the true breaker.
Quiver in your boots, quaker.
Looking at the shaker.

This be our tuning.
Our pruning.
Out of the assuming.
Glooming.

The seal has been broken.
It has been spoken.
The dead awoken.
Hear it, this not misspoken.

Rise to renew.
The Kingdom pursue.
Peace we never knew.
Joy comes into view.

Righteousness, virtue.
Oh, I will tell.
No yell.
This place is where I dwell.
Opposite of my personal hell.
Where I fell.

The deep of my soul.
I thought there was a hole.
However, the One on patrol.
Showed me the scroll.

Let's go for a stroll.
Up over the knoll.
Show what was stole.

A new role.
New goal.
Give me your whole.
Up to you to enroll.

Plight

Being led by the dazzling bright.
Down many roads out of sight.
It's right.
This plight.

To some it may seem a flight.
Though maybe slight.

It's my delight.
To have walked the trial in the night.
With only a flashlight.
To have been so cold, almost frostbite.
Brought a knife to a gunfight.
Tasted marmite.
Known outright.
Wore skintight.
Worked for the sound bite.
Won a penlight.
Been frozen with stage fright.
Ran a stoplight.
Stared in wonder through the skylight.
Asked to rewrite.
Painted many a room off-white.
Been told to sit tight.
Watched a prizefight.
Loved in lamplight.
Fought a war with fire blight.
Had insight.
Taught to be polite.
Chased myself in twilight.

Had the shine of a knight.
Sat upright.
Traveled a fortnight.
All right.

It's been a sight.
More than quite.
This journey, my birthright.

Here now I write.
Under a searchlight.
Fight.
Trying to unite.
The thoughts, invite.
Out of sight.
Into the light.

Proceed

In days such as these.
We all feel the squeeze.
We've been asked to freeze.
From the wheeze and the sneeze.
From the rod and the reed.
From the disease.
By many decrees.
Bringing much unease.

Let's get on our knees.
Please.
Ask for mercy, healing, peace—plead.
We are in need.
We need to be freed.
From the feeling of being treed.
By a giant stampede.
From the weed and the greed.
Protect us from the words we've heard and misread.
Many an obstacle does impede.
Let's not concede.
Fear and uncertainty need to recede.
Of a different path lead.
With desperation and speed.
Water your seed.
Long for a new succeed.
Get down, get low, intercede.
A new creed.
To heed.

Are we willing to bleed?
Not all is guaranteed!
However, I say let's proceed.

Ripple

Sound the bell.
You are the ripple in the place you dwell.
Beginning a chain reaction tough to quell.
Opening doors to the digging well.

There is much to say and tell.
A story being written, coming out of its shell.
Disqualifications must take a back seat, farewell.
Bringing revelations to new clientele.

Get on the soap box, yell!
This is a piece of the puzzle, this additional intel.
Taking to new heights, propel
Mining the details, foretell.

The sense, that feeling of unwell.
The bloating swell.
And sickening smell.
Gone it is, expel.

What is this understanding that does befell?
Indeed, the doors have opened, worthy compel.
Laying a new floor, impel.
Maybe, just maybe the prize, Nobel.

Speak

Into time.
Out of time.
Through time.
Chime.

In the daytime.
Nighttime.
Summertime.
Wintertime
Lunchtime.
Teatime.
Wartime.
Peacetime.
Bedtime.
Climb.

Part time.
Full time.
Half time.
Playtime.
Overtime.
Any time.
Rhyme.

Sometime,
To the grime,
The slime,
The crime.

The long, long line.
Even the divine.
Probably more than nine.
Assign.

Those in confine.
Decline.
Out of align.
The ones malign.
Need refine.
About to resign.
On the decline.

What of the wine?
The dine?
The fine?
The sign?
Ones enshrine.

What of the ones that pine?
Lost their shine?
No spine.
Tied up in twine.

Reassign,
Recombine,
Redesign,
Redefine.

It's seedtime.
Showtime.
Get ready for the incline.
Old-time.

So, climb.
Into your prime.
No more mime.
Worth more than a dime.
I'm!

Spoken

Words spoken.
Awaken the broken.
More than just token.
Sometimes prod and poke'n.
Cause and awoken.
Just soaken!

Do their part.
Get in your heart.
Impart.
Restart.

The sound.
Releases the bound.
The wound.
The drowned.

Listen to the tune.
Carefully hewn.
Warm like June.
Never too soon.
Off to the moon.
Swoon.

The song of a friend.
Beautiful blend.
Starting a new trend.
Transcend.

Thoughts from my dad.
Deepen and add.
Wash away the bad.
The sad.
The mad.
Just a tad.
Pull on your glad.

Walking in sync.
In a wink.
Without a blink.
Take it in, drink.
Pause and think.

The book is alive.
No need to strive.
More than survive.
Out of the nosedive.
No need to contrive.
Connive.
Feel deprive.
Much more than a test drive.

This collaborative.
Is determinative.
I forgive!
Outlive.
Live.

Surround

Walk the path nobody goes.
Be willing to try the narrow road, follow your nose.
Do you smell rose?

Trust shall be your companion.
Love will be your Champion.

A light will guide you.
Surround you.
Be above you.
Below you.
Before you.
Behind you.
Move when you move.
Wait for you.
Go on ahead of you.

To show the briar and thorn.
The stones in early morn.
Go ahead, this shall be your norm.
Make you, mold you into a new form.
You were created for this, it's why you were born.

Tension

What is the glue.
That holds the two.
Tighter than a screw.
Threw and through.

Two ends.
Blend.
Not possible to upend.
Offend.

Recommend.
Comprehend.
Apprehend.
Reap a dividend.

Buy in.
With a grin.
Twin.
Away from weak and thin.

Black, white.
Dim, bright.
Day, night.
Left, right.

Here hold the answers, willing to fight.
Higher than a kite.
To the highest height.
Out of sight.

Out on the edge.
With no hedge.
Just a ledge,
A pledge,
And a willingness to dredge.

Answers mend.
For family, for friend.
Defend.

The intend.
Of more than trends.
They will be penned.

The Beginning of First

Out on the scene burst.
This compulsion to go first.
Almost never rehearsed.
Dive in headfirst, immersed.

Let me be clear.
At the premier.
I probably will not bring up the rear.
It's the frontier!

Out in the lead.
Spreading out the seed.
The wind in your hair, love the speed.
Come with me your creed.
Paying no mind to fear, heed.
Let's do this deed.
After you can read.

The start.
Comes from the heart.
In whole and in part.
Shows as fine art.

The initiate.
May need an officiate.
To propitiate.
Conciliate.
Some lines delineate.

In the begin.
The when.
Does spin.
It's there within.

The lead release.
An invitation of peace.
Become its mouthpiece.
Settle down take out a lease.
Saying no to decrease.
Just forever increase.

The Hook

Thinking of what's the next look.
Drawing on the experiences, partook.
What will be the hook?

The strategy? Use the rook.
Thoughts mix with words, bubbling as a brook.
This is what was undertook.

Past the bend crook.
Hidden in a computer nook.
Up the river, home, as the chinook.

Nothing being overlook.
Grabbing the opportunity, took.
Thoughts on the hook.

Paper and pen shook.
It was a slow cook.
But none the less, here is the book.

The Call

There I lay.
At an end of a day.
Further back in time I must say.
My young life feeling full of disarray.
With tears on full display.
A voice said, "Hey!"
"I love you!" It said, "Convey."
It took me away.
On a journey, stay.
Never will I forget that day.

The Cave

These are the multiple compounding days,
Lingering off of my page.
Speaking to me,
Encouraging a disengage.

Such is the life in the cave,
Longing for an exchange.
The numbing wonder,
Fully engaged.

The home that I made,
Here in this cage.
What seems like years,
Difficult with rage.

Is this not the training of the sage?
Taking the backstage.
Fully engulfed,
In taking very little wage.

However, the inner voice caged,
Is feeling the age.
And is wanting out,
To gauge.

Here we go, time to embrace what's pained,
And recognize the war waged.
Here is the greatness,
Of the interchange.

Send out the page.
Going to a new stage!
Out in the light,
Into a season of change.

The Fab Four

Oh, what is in store?
I see the more.
And the greater more.
My ceiling is your floor.

I know the questions of destiny and purpose.
Great they are! Even fabulous.
Remember the source.
It is the greatest resource.

Watched you grow.
Come into a flow.
Of love, mercy, and go.
I release and take off my whoa.

There is no greater time than now.
I believe you will watch many a knee bow.
You will be protected from the pow and the ow.
You will look back on an unbelievable, how?

It is a thrill.
To watch your will.
And there is less and less for me to fill.
I see many stories of the mill and till.
That you will fully fill.

All of you will know the power.
All of you will have your own tower.
None of you will duck or cower.
You will all succeed in the hour.

My love for you is great!
It fills my plate.
Here, there is no wait.
And you all know at this rate, tears will continue to be part of my state.

It makes me grin.
To think of the where you've been.
Better than apples in a bin.
Love is the win.

The One

A Man.
In a chair.
Sitting.
Peaceful.
Loving.
Sure.
Overflowing.
Wise.
Piercing.
Strong.
Ready.
Patient.
Holy.
Trusting.
Exposing.
Experienced.
Faithful.
Beautiful.
Measured.
Timely.
Understanding.
Compassionate.
Merciful.
Full.
Complete.
Knowing.
Judge...
All.

The Ploy

I figured part of it out.
No doubt.
Started early as a sprout.

What is this drought!
Potential burnout!
Give me the buyout.
The closeout.

This knockout.
It's throughout.
Lookout.
Desire to checkout.
Get to a hideout.
So not to blackout.

What is the ploy?
The decoy?
The employ?
To bring to the edge of destroy.

This attempt to steal joy.

Almost a coup.
Before I got a clue.
Tried to screw.
All I did accrue.
Hard work hue.
What a zoo.
Need a new view.

I felt slapped.
Strapped.
Tapped.
I snapped.
Realizing the fact
After the hack.
This illegal act.
All of me, it did impact.
By a giant distract.
Sometimes abstract.

Time to retract.
Use different tact.
Sign a new contract.

A new delivery.
Has a history.
Even antiquity.
Mystery.
Definitely not elementary.
Makes your insides glittery,
Jittery.
Always in your periphery.
This victory.

The Rhythm of Words

Stirred up to write, paper and pen.
These words all stored up, hibernating, den.
Waiting for the right time of when.
To make their debut before many women and men.

What be their purpose, their reason, their contend?
Will they apprehend?
Revelation comprehend?
Newness descend.

Sentence, paragraph into verse.
Clarity of thoughts immerse.
Much coffee and tea disperse.
Burning the midnight oil traverse.

Finding a rhythm form.
Late through the night till morn.
This not be the norm.
However, this hard work will cause the transform.

Come to the place of create.
Lift off the blockage and weight.
Line up the thoughts, editor straight.
Comma, period, colon, partake.

The binding does link.
The paper sync.
There it be all fresh in ink.
So, pour yourself that refreshing drink.

The Shake

The shaking has shown us.
To take notice.
Of the history ferocious.
Hopefully provoke us.

We pray for the arrival,
Of a revival.
One worthy of archival.

This is the generation,
For reformation.
We are the location.

A new Renaissance,
Will be the response.
In our culture, ensconce.

I see the orders.
Being shot out like mortars.
To all the transformers.

Decrees to govern.
From east, west, north, southern.
Discovered,
And uncovered.

As chaos ensues.
With many a view,
And oh, so much news.

A process will show.
It will grow,
Like fresh bread dough.

Fresh as a new morning snow.
It may start slow,
But continue it will flow.

Rhyme and verse will be sung.
From the old and the young.
From every nation, every tongue.

New gates swung.
New art hung.
New rings rung.
New springs sprung.
All of us one.
Heroes unsung.

After the bumps have been smoothed.
All the information pooled.
Viewed,
And reviewed.
And stamped approved.
What will be our conclude?

The Way Out

We all need a good laugh.
A quote, an engrave, oh yeah, an epigraph.
So, on behalf.
Of my gaffe.
Armed with a bar graph.
Raise the carafe.

To my thoughts, they sometimes feel like chaff.
But reach toward new heights, my friend giraffe.

Grab the shaft.
Of the staff.
The one you did craft.
Your whole, not half.

These words do submit.
To bridle and bit.
Worked on the wit.
Did not quit.
Went to the pit.
To be refit.
Must not omit.

On the way out.
Found a new route.
With a little pout.
Did spout.
However, gained some clout.
In this drought.

There must be a respond.
In this upward beyond.
Correspond.
Then, it dawned.

Review the scan.
The plan.
You know, the one from Stan.
Or was it, Dan?
Peter Pan?
Doesn't matter, it came at the beginning of this race, ran.
The one from your clan.
The biggest fan.
It says you are a new man.

East to West

Move we did to a place far, far away.
In the late of April, early May.
Taking the risk with balance and weigh.
Twenty-four months wrestling is nothing to downplay.

It was noon on that day.
Yes, it was a Saturday.
The truck all packed, ready to make hay.
Everything in so tightly so nothing could sway.

Time to get underway.
The beckoning of the highway.
Lines white and yellow in full array.
Glowing, showing the way.

I dare say.
This is no ballet.
Traffic did bring some delay.
Brake lights, potholes, and debris caused some dismay.

Nonetheless, most often felt as if lifted above the disarray.
And carried as if in a miraculous valet.
Kinda like a living screenplay.
The best I can portray.

Through long straightaway.
High mountain skyway.
Ocean's sea spray.
On and on till we did come to the state, C.A.

Off the freeway.
Met with the welcome of a shining ray.
No need to pay.
Off you go, this fine getaway.

Through the valleys where buffalo lay.
The forests fray.
Weaving up and around a mountain, grey.
Even a little snow on display.

Four thousand miles is a very long pathway.
A virtual ash fault buffet.
Seven-day relay.
This journey, adventure, obey.

What a trip we did slay.
Beautiful as a rainbow bouquet.
This east to west survey.
Let's do it all over again, hooray.

Then

Time, tic toc, tic toc.
Rushes slowly bye like a sloth.
What's wrong with this clock?
Please get some batteries in stock.
When will escape happen from this crock.
More than a walk.
I want mach.

Then, realization hits.
More clues I need to unlock.
This sluggish unrelenting knock.
Where is the block?
Can I get a new place to dock?

Then, after many a pulled-up sock
And a clean-up of sideway chalk.

I hear…far more beautiful than Bach.
Higher than highest flock.
The sounds interlock.
Blows open the box.
Causing an interior shock.
I almost can't believe, I want to bock.
Quicker than a fox.
More patience than a croc.

Here we go, release the lock.
It calls.
Whispers.
Squeaks.

Yells.
Sings
And, speaks.
I am the Rock!

To You

To you.
There's nothing left to prove.
It's time to make that move.
Needing...
The need, the approve.

There's nothing here, and I'm oft surrounded by empty thoughts in my head.
It makes me so tired because round and round they go...
Is there nothing else instead?

Waking early,
Wondering.
Pondering.
Discussing.
Discerning.
Thinking.
Blinking.
Yearning.
Turning.
Burning.

Here, standing on the balcony of truth.
Overlooking.
Peering deep into my youth.

Then.
There He is!
So gentle.
Governmental.

Joyful.
Royal.
Patient.
Loyal.
Faithful
Expectant.
Experienced.
Respected.

Loving.
And buzzing!

The feelings are overcoming.
Fearless.
Yet so ever near us.
Compassionate.
Deeply kind.
With a love never blind.

Fully merged by the tears and the blood He shed.
All of regal and royal, with a crown full of jewels on His head.
Perfect and pure, His death was for me and you instead.

I'm full.

Transit

Stuck between the now and then.
Feels like year ten.
Where I said, "Amen."
Better get a pen.

Write my way out of this transition.
Gaining and gaining toward an ignition.
To this, sometimes veiled mission.
Hope-filled position.

The answer was yes.
Nonetheless.
At the end of the address.
Responding to the mess.
Express.

I had been blinded.
By what my sight had provided.
The message excited.
Spoke to the deep, reminded.

The pain in the change.
Sometimes be strange.
I know not these feeling, derange.
Estrange.
Yet, having great range.

Active action, awaken.
Get to make'n.
Even while shaken.

The assignment needs taken.
This contest.
The one, your quest.
Get at it with your best.
Zest.
Here, be blessed.

Weigh

Love won the day.
Knelt down and pray.
Thanks on display.
Was the main convey.
Cry in full array.
With the purpose of sway.
Many thoughts to weigh.

The atmosphere thick.
It happened so quick.
Roads were slick.
Swerving enough to make one sick.
All felt like a trick.
Like getting hit upside the head with a brick.

The snake is dead.
Saw its strangled head.
On a mantel spread.
Unable anymore to bring dread.
Fear was its bread.
Suspicion the main thread.
Put it to bed.
Enough said.

Settle the dust.
With all that was thrust.
In upheaval, disgust.
Refiled by unjust
Need to make an adjust.
Relearn how to trust.

This is a must.
Come to find out, there were many of us all.
Who didn't drop the ball.
Set up a wall.
With a call.
United, standing tall.

As memories of the event grow old.
Stories will be told.
Of the bold.
Who would not be controlled.
Sold.

Words

Words spoken.
Sometimes bent, broken.
Release a flood of emotion.
Unlock present, past, future, open.

Words create.
Make.
Break.
Drive into the ground the proverbial stake.

Words shake.
Take.
Awake.
Change what we do, our old life forsake.

Words speak.
Seek.
Critique.
Bring on new technique.

Words bring.
Ring.
Sing.
The crowing of a new King.

Words improve.
Move.
Remove.
Sign on the line, you're approved.

Words cause.
Pause.
Laws.
Unlocking many jaws.

Words fill.
Mill.
Drill.
Bring money into the till.

Words date.
Relate.
Debate.
Stand in the court and set things straight.

Words complete.
Greet.
Meet.
Bring new life, heartbeat.

Words.

Seat

At the door of our desire.
The door of higher.
Here, there is no fire.
Here, no mire.
Here, you will not tire.

Come to the seat.
All here complete.
Feel the love, heat.
Peace unable to beat.
Impossible defeat.
Gold on the street.
Here is where we meet.
A giant table, a feast.

Up here higher. Oh, the peace on repeat.
Where words meet.
And thoughts become your treat.
Together sprout and grow as the wheat.

Up here higher above the line.
The snake, serpent, and their kind.
Pay them no mind.
Come up here and unwind.

Here is where we imagine and dream.
Breaking the curses, redeem.
Unlocking truth stream.
Rise to the top cream.

The seat is the truth.
Reviving your youth.
Reforming structure and booth.
Bringing the ability to get long in the tooth.

Whether a recliner, pew, or chair.
Try to not be put in a square.
But be fully aware.
Of your who, what, when, where.

Where We Begin

When the wall fails, falls.
Open and vulnerable to more, the all.
It messes with the scales.
Eliminating the guards and rails.

Out oozed.
The cause is confused.
Feeling abused.
Not too amused

What from within,
This was allowed in.
Was it sin?
Where to begin?

My friend, my friend!
It was near the end.
Lost in protection much time we did spend.
Leaving holes, no way to defend.

Armed with an understanding gain.
Revelation obtain.
Relieving the strain.
On new terrain.

It's here in this place.
Give lots of grace.
It's a journey not a race.
So, set the pace.

Now new boundaries can create.
On a completely new slate.
Set the record straight.
Remember the old as we eat from this new plate.

Window

The thought of me and you, an opening to pass through.
Mainly a tool.
Often the crowning jewel.
Lining up to get a view.

The bringer of light.
Even a glimmer in the night.
Can be quite the sight.
The dancing excite.

Sitting by the sill.
All dressed in twill.
Observing my hill.
Awaiting a much needed refill.

Thoughts gather as leaves.
Fallen from their trees.
Making one believe.
There's more than what seems.

Move the curtain aside.
Here be my abide.
Going along for a ride.
Taking it all in stride.

A need for what's clear.
To bring a necessary steer.
The ones of merry and cheer.
Signs read, *here.*

Offering protection from the wind and rain.
Sunlight strain.
In beauty dusk wain.
This pane.

Ride

A dim light inside.
Made itself known, cried.
Has me all twisted, tied.
Needing to be applied.
Longing a companion beside.
Waiting for a decide.
Knowing it will not be denied.
Yearning for a guide.
To go on a ride.

Everything now points.
To the aching of the joints.
Here a fear of disappoint.
Has bathed me, anoint.

This ride or journey if you will.
Has no excuses, none, nil.
Swallow the pill.
It shall be settled in the calm and the still.
Here, all the sickness and ill.
Will be put on the grill.

New life, instill.
It will more than refill.
A roller coaster thrill.
Purpose and destiny, it shall fulfill.

Voice

Lots of messages out there, voices trying.
In misery, crying.
Sinister and lying.
Unjustly implying.
lost, in the sighing.
Unconditionally, dying.
On the edge defying.
Secretly spying.
Future, eyeing.
Forever, prying.
Tired of complying.
Looking for some providing.

The voice matters.
In the splatter.
The clatter.
In the pitter and patter.
The scatter.
One will arise above the chatter.

Okay, listen.
Sit down and take a position.

Feeling the glisten.
This beautiful condition.

Mulitiplica(tion).
Not just addition.

Parting the partition.
Smashing the suspicion.
Giving full admission.
To this perfect acquisition.

Unbelievable definition.
In this wonderful collision.

Send out the transmission.
No opposition.

More magical than the greatest magician.
More technical than the techiest technician.
Smarter than the smartest mathematician.

Bring out the proposition.
This new edition.
The ultimate expedition.
Having all permission.

Love the ignition.
The voice the mission.

Needing Work

Sitting in my home.
Thankful in a comfortable hone.
Able to view the snow, no phone.
Free to roam.
Drinking coffee with foam.
Hopefully not outgrown.

However, sometimes prone.
To groan.
To moan.
To the door shown.
Put away the stone.
So easily thrown.

Hear the tone?
To be Known.
To BE known.
To BE KNOWN.
No more be alone.

Let's dethrone.
This ingrown.
Headphone.
Cyclone.

No postpone.
Bury the loan.
At the gravestone.

Own.
A new throne.
With the flag flown.
Sewn.
Out of the all the seeds grown.
A stepping stone.
To a new zone.

Renew

When the Christmas lights dim.
You know it's probably time for the gym.
The cold is already old, and winter starts off feeling grim.
You're ready for a tropical swim.

Preserve the view.
Engage the pursue.
Eliminate what's untrue.
Set your mind to renew.
Persevere for what's due.
Remember the review.
Vision to hue.

For, when the page turns.
It's time to learn.
Maybe a burn.
Deepen the yearn.
Satisfy your concern.
And quiet the churn.

With all that the year brought.
It caused much thought.
Let's continue to burn hot.
And fight where we ought.

Off the Shelf

I see a light that's been taken off the shelf.
It was high up, off by itself.
Up there, gaining understanding, wisdom, and stealth.
Now moved into a different position where it can be seen and felt.
Here, in a new position, many will see its great wealth.

Whispered West

All I Need

Ever Feel This Way?

Fourteen

Winter

The Hook

East to West

Ride

Finishing Thoughts

The expression of words through poetry is a unique way to communicate. The creativity it offers is most often beautiful. Sometimes simple. Thought provoking. Jarring and challenging. I love the latitude it offers to be creative in expressing an idea or concept. As a creative, poetry is wonderful.

Poetry challenges our thinking, mindsets, and beliefs. Poetry brings clarity. Poetry stirs us up. All of these, I have experienced. Even as I reread my work, I experience wonder and amazement with the challenges they offer.

It has been a joy to share some of my journey through my worded wonders with you. As you have been able to peer into my story through these poems, I trust that you have been challenged. I hope you laughed. I hope you have been provoked.

About the Author

Author and creative Peter Eisses's journey gives him a unique perspective. World travelers, he and his wife Lisa, of 30+ years, presently call Redding, California, home and have served with missional and creative hearts in many different spheres of influence.

As a farmer and one with an inventive mind, the life lessons from his farming background flow in his writing. Mixing the creative with farming and other life events—regular and grand—brings a fresh and new perspective to the poetry expression. Peter loves the creative process and this shines through in his writing—challenging us to think outside the box, bringing new thoughts, ideas, and potential freedoms.

Connect with Peter:
Email: **whisperedwest@gmail.com**
Facebook: **www.facebook.com/peter.eisses.7**
Instagram: **@peter_eisses_**
Website: **www.petereisses.com**
YouTube: **www.youtube.com/@PeterEisses**

Printed in Great Britain
by Amazon